Mayflower Voyage
400 Year Anniversary
1620 - 2020

Creative Advisor; Andrew J. MacLachlan

Cover Creator & Illustrator; Bonnie S. MacLachlan © 2019

Editor; Susan Sweet MacLachlan

ISBN: 9781089022381

BookN.it Publications
BookNitPublications.com
BookNitPublications@iCloud.com
Griswold, Ct

(Name) _____

Mayflower Passenger
1620

Polly Doane

Mother — Mary Ann 1789-1870
Kenosha

Father — Daniel Bronson 1786-1858
(AGE 40) Loraine, OH

1818 - Lucy Clark Bronson — Columbiana Ohio

1819 - Martha Doane Bronson 1819-1896

1822 - Betsy Anne Bronson — Columbiana OH 1822-1848

1824 Mercy Carey Bronson D. Madison Wisconsin 1918
M. 1853 Racine, Wisconsin
"Charles Henry Comstock"

1827 Alfred Bronson 1827-1827 Euclid, Oh

1830 Cary Solon Bronson The Twin 1830-1895 Euclid
1863 m. Sarah Jane Carpenter D 1895 Kenosha, Wisc Ohio
1879 m. Fannie Avann

1830 Aurora Bronson Twin (1830-1830) Euclid

1839
1869 M. Amasa Morgan (Lucy was 21)
1818-1867

Dedications

This notebook is dedicated to my family and all
the families that risked their lives to travel
to America, in search of a better life.

If You are a beginner or professional Genealogist
Mayflower Descendant, or simply enjoy family history
and want a special place to keep track of your notes
or research, then this is the notebook for you!

#NoteBooksThatTravel

The Mayflower Compact

(Modern Version)

IN THE NAME OF GOD, AMEN. We, whose names are underwritten, the Loyal Subjects of our dread Sovereign Lord King James, by the Grace of God, of Great Britain, France, and Ireland, King, Defender of the Faith, etc..

Having undertaken for the Glory of God, and Advancement of the Christian Faith, and the Honour of our King and Country, a Voyage to plant the first Colony in the northern Parts of Virginia: Do by these Presents, solemnly and mutually, in the Presence of God and one another, covenant and combine our-selves together into a civil Body Politick, for our better Ordering and Preservation, and Furtherance of the Ends aforesaid: And by Virtue hereof do enact, constitute, and frame, such just and equal Laws, Ordinances, Acts, Constitutions, and Officers, from time to time, as shall be thought most meet and convenient for the general Good of the Colony unto which we promise all due Submission and Obedience.

IN WITNESS whereof we have here-unto sub-scribed our names at Cape-Cod the eleventh of November, in the Reign of our Sovereign Lord King James, of England, France, and Ireland, the eighteenth, and of Scotland the fifty-fourth, Anno Domini; 1620.

John Carver	William White	Edward Fuller	Gilbert Winslow
William Bradford	Richard Warren	John Turner	Edmond Margeson
Edward Winslow	John Howland	Francis Eaton	Peter Brown
William Brewster	Stephen Hopkins	James Chilton	Richard Britteridge
Isaac Allerton	Edward Tilly	John Crackston	George Soule
Myles Standish	John Tilly	John Billington	Richard Clarke
John Alden	Francis Cooke	Moses Fletcher	Richard Gardiner
Samuel Fuller	Thomas Rogers	John Goodman	John Allerton
Christopher Martin	Thomas Tinker	Degory Priest	Thomas English
William Mullins	John Rigdale	Thomas Williams	Edward Doty
			Edward Leister

The original document has been lost, so the exact wording is uncertain. Historic documents differ slightly in capitalization, spelling, punctuation and wording. The signers names differ in spelling from source to source.

400 Anniversary 1620 - 2020

Mayflower Voyage

FINDING YOUR ROOTS

OPB 1/10/23

SALEM ~~CIVIL WAR~~ WITCH TRIALS

Thomas Chandler 1656

Battle of Lexington 1775
Conc

Mayflower 1620
Massachusetts Bay Colony
Economic + religious turmoil

* 1692 Essex Co Mass — Salem Witch Trials

Thomas Chandler - tell young people their fortunes
   Testified

(social outcast) Hanged
fortune → Samuel Wardwell
teller
testimony → Thomas Chandler

Jeff's 8th
great grand
father

1692 Sept
Thomas
Chandler
→ Testified

(widow of 10)
Mary Parker) — Hanged
Andover
Arts - Wickedly vs. Sarah Phelps
+ Hannah Bigsby of Andover
Hannah Chandler (daughter)
Sarah Phelps (grand daughter)

Francis ~~Dayton~~ Dane (Brother in Law of
        Thomas Chandler)
      (Protect his brother
      in law)

only person who signed petition didn't have
a person accused of witch craft   MOBS
a place people go to take a break
from their conscience.

2

Witchcraft
Finding Your Roots

CLARE DANES

Salem   Born 1616   Margaret Scott — one of last
hanged 1692   VICTIMS
Sept 1692   — accused of Witchcraft

memorial   — accused by neighbor of
bench
1992   killing cows

            — neighbors 10 testified
            against impoverished widow

            — hung
1710   18 yrs after execution
        made restitution

        risky to be associated even if innocent
        Margaret's daughter was dead

2

26

37

3

54

57

4

70

Mayflower Voyage

5

6

Mayflower Voyage

Mayflower Voyage

Mayflower Voyage

Mayflower Voyage

Mayflower Voyage

Made in the USA
Monee, IL
25 January 2022

89806488R00069